linguistick
uistickling

© Enrique Enriquez
  & EyeCorner Press | 2013

linguistick
uistickling

Published by EYECORNER PRESS
August 2013
Roskilde

ISBN: 978-87-92633-25-5

Cover design and layout: Camelia Elias

Printed in the US and UK

linguistick
uistickling

enrique enriquez

EYECORNER PRESS

linguistick
uistickling
enrique enriquez

"I refuse to accept any alphabetic display as final"

Ezra P un
o d

Index

pun

calembour *(c - ale + mb - o + u - s = cambur:*
whose peeled skin makes the tongue slip)

jeu de mots *(moth play/juego de polillas/jogo borboletas)*
juego de palabras *(jugo de palabras/word juice/suco de palavras)*

gioco di parole *(words on parole)*

trocadilhos *(trocar/taroccare*
carcerato)

wortspiel *(word-spell)*
ordspill *(words spill/word's peel/concha de palabras*
conch: as in back of the ear
kissing the c)

retrouvécano *(you can't believe in words if you are going to play with*
them)

hieroglyphs
anomaly = *langue verte*
(each image would be a variance of the preceding one.
color becomes an unit for the measurement of time)

homophony
syzygy = *langue des oiseaux*

(each image would exist in a straight-line configuration with its analogical
equivalents.
color becomes visual glue)

anagrams

clinamen = *guy sçavoir*

(each image would contain the means of its own derailment.
color becomes cool r)

WARNING:

THE WIND CARRIED IT IN ITS BELLY (VOWELS)

THE EARTH IS ITS NURSE (CONSONANTS)

Enrique Enriquez

Each Friday, sometimes Thursday, I look in my inbox and often find Glee

Not that anyone should find that surprising in

Retrospect, or was that introspect, or am I a mere spectator

In EE's never-ending Tarot reading, often an exercise in semi-

Quiet punning, not running anywhere, not even *on the spot*, with rabid Q-

Uestions about the meaning of even the smallest word in situ

Everything falls into place

Each Friday, sometimes Thursday, I look in my inbox to discover more

Nuance than most conventional novels, as if when

Reading a narrative my mind strays to the page's edge further

Into notions of song and truth and reverie and epiphany with some anti-

Quated version of the big picture reduced to single syllables not req-

Uired to explain anything but this man's particular astonishment -- as if you

Entered a room full of light merely to extinguish it for more

Zen foods on the side of a New York delivery truck with its door ajar in Oz

                                        Victor Coleman

,Y

The goal of wordplay is the freedom to make it. The pleasure one feels while unpacking the ambivalence between the familiar and the unfamiliar side of words transcends the humorous aspect of puns. One has to handle words like a snake charmer, with a sense of boldness that always includes respect, for words can turn back unexpectedly and bite you. Wordplay deals with the way the eye hears what the ear sees.

A good symbol for wordplay would be a crab. In these games language doesn't move forward with the linear aplomb of a sentence but it scurries sideways in small incremental deviations. Anagrams refract the sound-sense of one word into separate syllables. Homophony extends these broken phonemes to the level of whole new words, making the game endless.

Wordplay is the no man's land where the schizophrenic and the mystic meet to exchange shirts. Who dares to remain shirtless? It is only if you believe in keys that you will find locks. Once opened they reveal the secrets no one kept (all texts carry a code that will be encrypted in the future, when someone other than their author finds what wasn't left in there). Through our acroamatic acrobatics we refuse to let ourselves be lured by the currency of language. The very act of reading seems impossible. When the curve of the eye kisses the flatness of letters words become either concave or convex. The wet surface of our bodies, our eyeballs and lips, confronts the dryness of the page. All things, once wet, change their color. To become labial is to become labile. This is the reason why any word can slip and become a pun.

enrique enriquez, New York, 2013

a bone grammar* is a

bonne gramm**aire**

c ielo *œil*

seeelo sk**eye**

eye/eye/*oreille*/**ear**th

lang**ue**

laᴜe

l'eau

the ice

open the**m out**

NOTE:

to make

light   bounce

a color

against   a white

surface

in a grimoire a word spelled becomes matter

HORSE is SCYTHE plus ROAD

( )ever ( )ook ( )ack

SOUL is HOUSE plus OWL

words are a poor substitute for stones:

two **STONE**s make **SENSE**
three **STONE**s make **NONSENSE**

two **STONE**s make a **NEST**
three **STONE**s make **ONENESS**

  stone
+ stone
——————
sonnet

BREAD and WATER to make a TEAR
SALT and MILK to make SILK
BREAD and SALT to make a BREAST
a TWIRL of WATER and MILK

(**METAL** is WATER
and MILK is **TIME**)

FOOL is COFFIN

and CLOUD is **IF**

NOTE: fool equals coffin plus cloud, but a cloud isn't a fool's coffin.

a grim oar:

stone teeth.
In the beginning all letters where finger puppets.
In the beginning numbers where dance steps.

    K__N _Y_
    _EE_ E_E

iron teeth.
A bird's skin is pierced by feathers

The
s,(*υεwεμs* = shaman)'s necklace

    ah αυe   ane ye
    pυe μe   ah and
    υe we   am an
    p(r)o me aw ord

(After Walter van Beirendonck)

wood teeth.
To make FIRE:

Tattoo a dragon on an o(ra)n(ge)
            on on an o   n

Squee(ze it).

NOTE: I could say all kind of annoying things if my mouth were (blu)r(red).

Oh, a fabled gesturing!

V as in bird

V as in c(up), (unt), womb

I as in dick

Y as in fuck

Language of the birds

NOTE: Love-making is one of those intriguing moments when somebody-else believes in you more than you believe in yourself.

un.

sound is physic(all) voice is body. whosign?

lan.

pert(ur)bations in o(ur) eard(ru)ms

vowel is bowel voice is clapper body's bell body is drum

image is consonant eye is vowel ear drums

gua.

before seeing the light tongue moves in the dark

ran out of tongue's cream ran out of tongue, scream

(er)ase a suff(er)ing

to find the next one

(to make a tongue: mix food, bodies, trees, birds and water, b(on)ding
and bel(on)ging: bell on gin)

ged.

music and myth - musi   m th = candy man created god to avoid accidents

I am happy, I don't dream

but you can if you ( )ry

we

THE SKIN IS THE BOUNDARY OF THE SYMBOLIC UNIVERSE

desire

TO UNDERSTAND THE *MEN BRAIN*

what

DON'T BOTHER WITH RATTLES AND DRUMS

language

IT MAY BE GOOD TO CARRY A FEATHER IN YOUR POCKET

wants

BUT IT PAYS BETTER TO PRETEND YOU DO

surviv**(al is)** a strugg**(le f)**or symbols

are forebodings a natu**(ral ph)**enomenon?

(or is that just gossip?)

language IS A BODY *we spell* IN ORDER *to inhabit* IT

L E T T E R S A R E P E R E N N I A L R E P O S I T O R I E S O F E N E R G Y

MATTER IS THE SYMBOL FOR THOUGHT:

O　　N

I

O　　N

onion

on I on

on e on

on & on
oh! neon!

a D oubt
a second thought
a D is a square becoming a circle

One same body: DRM
for DRUM
and DREAM.

To find laughter in ALPHABET:

remove the first three letters counting forward
remove the first three letters counting backward

NOTE: *for a merrier effect read the remaining letters aloud, three or more times.*

SIX-POINTED STAR

(or how to make a bird)

BIRD

MAN WANNA **WOMAN**

SUN ONUS **MOON**

UNBARS MIND   DOMAIN WOMB

MIND DOMAIN

UNBARS WOMB

NOTE: bold creates light.

ROSE *seer* **EAR**

sense (arcane) *fear*

NOSE *seance* **FACE**

NOTE: as quare is queer.

AQUA VITAE + TONGUE

=

VEGETATION (**VAGINA**)

to make a fish:

( )low your ( )owels

in an aquarium

AQUA VITAE + HEART

=

THEATRE **(HEAT)**

(an image won't hold your voice)

AQUA VITAE + HAND

=

IDEA (**HINTED**)

(if you can't find a syntax buy a suit)

AQUA VITAE + BODY

=

BEAUTY (**TOYED**)

NOTICE: fill your pockets with stones and offer them to people when they ask you about the whether.

b) lack **c)** row

w) hit **e) s)** wan

p) e **a)** cock

p) hoe **n)** ix

NOTE:

alchemy my leach
solve et coagula loves actual ego
prima materia I am a prime rat
albedo et rubedo rude taboo bleed
nigredo ignored
philosopher stone hot help poisoners

bonjour   o o

conjure con-jour   o   o   o

light of hand   o

      oiseau
        eau
        sea
     oui!

NOT(ic)E: a need is the first half of a needle.
         if you loose the needle you will find the haystack.

NOT ICE: the avoidance of the period can be accomplished when the rules of syntax are applied grammatically and logically to an unbroken sentence,
         or by taking the pill.

on the ground a stone is a stone/

words often take the shape of birds, small objects, or other animals

in your hand a stone is a bird/

words constitute a speculative exploration of the material world

birds are the eyes of the sky/

words are hallucinogenic agents

in the sky a stone is a word/

ecstatic oral performance/the word is the w(o)und/the mouth is a hole through which the bird flies out/yawning helps to catch it back//he is a mediator between language and man/he eliminates that what is ordinary in language to access an ecstatic context/ his words are steel(still) arrows:

a **glossolalic,**

gloss-o-Lalique, speaks flowers: **gloss-o-lilac,**

to fake an angel:

he opens the w(o)und:

traum(a)/dream/drum

he heals the knife:

co(ul)eur/heart/hurt

he reattaches the tongue:

b(eau)té/oh!

s(ha! ha! ha! ha! ha! ha! ha! ha! ha! ha! ha! ha! ha! ha!)man

(gam)

eyes blink

(bo)

head nods

(ling)

brain waves

a superstition is a poetic license/

put the sound of a needle/in his water/

put the sound of *clove/wine/and pepper/*

put the knife above the key/the key above the stick/the stick above

the bones/the bones around the skull/

a

c ross

a   bove

a circl

e

a fried fish's eyes are wide open/and the fish can't see/

the fish cant' see/you put sweets under the tree/

and it bent it's knees/it bent it's knees/

you must know the name of words/a K won't make

a good hammer/a K would make a good ache/

an aitch won't ache if you swallow it/gotta know it's name/

<pre>
                    a

                c   s

              a   e

              a   l

               e
</pre>

cook the flying squirrel/eat the seven spots/crack the egg to see the spirits

in the gloss/the mouth is the earth/the tongue is the wind/

the tongue is the bree/

/dge/ch/between past and present.

NOTE: if you don't have lemons, make LE-MONDE.

towards
transparency : opaque
         things
must be *comme*
language

(w+ill) (s+he) (h+ave) (h+er)?
(w+ill+s) (he) (s+have) (he+r)?
(wi+ll) (she+sh) (ave) (he+re)?

all w in ds re turn to t he
moth er f eat her

WARNING: a word is a thought cut short.

paragrammantics, the
   mantic
    antics
of the praragrammatical,

where words refuse and then
    re fuse,
following the Mallarmean
     mean mirage
       age of rhyme-as-unity

(janus-like shapes eliciting a big-bang laughter)
It is the tarologist's job to know when to polk a dot.
this fact can be easily confirmed by finding the fool's footprints on
la maison diev,
a card that never should be called "the tower", since

la maison = *l'ame songe*

the fool stands on a puddle
the fool is followed by a poodle

puddle - poodle = od,
which it is.

la lvne: heaven cries over the sea
    cries   sea
      cry + *sea = crazy*

crazy = cray c (where **c** is the the visible part of that what is emerging above
the surface of the water)

                              c
                          marsh
                              r
                              a
                              b

NOTE:
     tarot
     torat
     thorax
      ho ax

the tarot is our
top rank

occhieggiare

o   egg   ege/eye   o

comer com os olhos

o   s ol

NOTE:
       o o
white c   tt n
       o   o
blue   p lka d ts

antidepress   blat   conson   dec
     ant   ant   ant   ant

eggpl   flagell   gesticul
  ant   ant   ant

hydr   irrit   jubil   lubric
 ant   ant   ant   ant

maidserv   nonirrit   oscul
   ant   ant   ant

piss   qu   relax   somnambul
ant   ant   ant   ant

tru   urtic   vocifer   w
ant   ant   ant   ant

NOTE: How much weight c an an an t carry?

1.
a man
a mano calda
ama
   an
     oca

XIIII.
the cant
    ti amo is
decantiamoci su
decant
   anti-a / ansia

3.
del più del meno
delpi   men

4.
tra il prima e il poi
trail   mail
  trama

NOTE: for every new possible combination of letters in a word a new state of being emerges:

to do or not to do

to door, not todo

TAXI DE(a)R MY BIRDS

1.

abc/a busy

/abe easy

abécédaire/ave sed aire/ave seda aire

/a B ce d'air

/ave céder/l'oiseaux céde/

l'oiseau abandonné/l'oiseau a band donné/

(*l'oiseau n'est pas un orchestre*)

abecedario/ave seda río/ave sed ario/

a vece, Darío

un pájaro no es la orquesta

/un pájaro no es la banda/un pájaro no es lavanda

/un pájaro nuez lavanda

el ave se da aire/

2.

/nightingale/night in gale

/night tingle/night thing le/

neigh teen glee/

NOTE: was so oiseau (s = snake / o = ouroboros)

   s s

     o o

   ss oo

when the sert enters the letter

she got **boobs** as big as **balloons**

       oo   oo

NOTE: The pattern oo   oo carries the analogical mapping (boobs-as-balloons) to it's limits.

It makes it irresistibly physical.

There is a cant, a song inside these words: boo/ba/boo/balloo...

In it we intuit four mouths singing in a chorus, or the matting call of the stag: ö ö ö ö...

René Guenón wrote: "the language of the birds, which can also be called "angelic language", and which is symbolized in the human world by rhythmic language, for the science of rhythm, which has many applications, is in fact ultimately the basis of all the means which can be brought into action in order to enter into communication with the higher states of being."

All rhythms bear the present of the present.

The present is our "higher state of being". (higher ogle if)

Rather than hoping for the language of the birds to account for a connexion with a metaphysical realm, we could see it as a means towards a 'pataphysical exploration of the physical world.

We don't wait for the angel to come down and talk to us, but following poet Christian Bök, we read "the angel in the angle".

NOTE TO THE NOTE: The word boob is a palindrome.

NOTE TO THE NOTE TO THE NOTE: The world qooq is also a palindrome, but it can't bounce.

NOTE TO THE NOTE TO THE NOTE TO THE NOTE: The word qooq is not a word.

NOTE TO THE NOTE TO THE NOTE TO THE NOTE TO THE NOTE: actual boobs are also palindromes.

B is a fist, and **K** is an open hand

(like two dots making a map

like two signpost making a road)

a **P** dipping its toes in a pond becomes an **R**

when the *escargot* sticks its head out, the **O** becomes a **Q**

some people keep the escargot's shells aside: a bag of letters **C**

if you and I make a toast with our **V**s, we will make a **W**

you can also make a **W** if you kill an **M**

(logomenics = loon's gem)

Speech:
Bureaucratic leash (+**leech**)
For the alphabet

I slept with a number **9** thinking it was a letter **g**

noncommunication is achieved
by turning around (180°)
the n, m, u and a,
like this:

uoucowwnuicetiou

NOTE: It is through noncommunication that the alphabet alert us to the actual circumstances of its being.

allegorical eye, all lie

  all deaf

hecate,

a higher ogle if

      i
encha n ed animalism/anim talism/talisman/i'm
       t

sore cry/sorcery

         phant asthma goria

        ha

chaos change/ ha   ha   /cha cha *son*/ ha   ha /cha cha *songe*
ha   ha /cha os cha nge/ ha ha /cha cha song/ ha ha

hint/   /yph
  /ogl/

tw
   inni = <u>unity</u>   .   *sang*   sang   .   liquor   *liqueur*
ng

tw
  in ni = <u>duality</u>   .   blood *chanté*   .   *le cœur*   licker
ng

NOTE: apart is one word suggesting duality that we take
       a part to suggest unity.

P.S.: The Bosse-de-Nage particle says: ha ha

to make a woman, a man

needs a **double you,**

and an **O.**

a **you** is an **I**

seen from the out

side, so: **W = I I**

inside of **O,** the sun

inside the moon, *la O*

es siempre ciclópea. **O**

mandor**la vulva**gina

al**monds** a(re d)oors

LEMON D LE MONDE

I rather punch

a whole in the hole:

I I = +

(**I I** also equals **V** and **X,** but never mind)

the **+** inside the **O**: man

dala/navel/*pati*

pemba/*vévé*/*wheel*

anima mania

demon monde

the infrathin ethernity of a escutcheon:

a heraldry of pubic hair.

NOTE: the wound in the side of Christ will be considered an act of plagiarism by anticipation from Lucio Fontana's Concetto Spaziale.

NOTE 2: M is as long as W

but nobody is as short as I

oo, o o

soon, solo

OO two bar
reled nos
trils
pa ir of bi no coo lar ey es

OO take a fut
off the but

OO take a ruth
off the tuth

feel powerfOOl

blow letters 'O'
inside a balloooooooooooooooooon
Until it pops

WARNING: don't let kids play with an O
they may fall inside

eo   *eo*   *eo*   *eo*   *eo*   *eo*

aj   cantal   cuchich   gorj   tit   zur

                                     iso   ino

                                   tr   tr

arri   *arru*   *ara*   *ra*

g   dura   llos p   po g   znido

                                    ul

                                   ul   ato

qui   ko   koe   ki

    qui   ko   ke   ke

ri   ri   le   ri

quí   ko   koe   ki

    o o   ho   hoo   eet   eet   itz   itz   ip   ip

pí pí coo koo tw   tw   tzv   tzv ch ch

NOTE: cajoleries, thro(At tar)t

                          's Conference of the birds (very much abridged)

cage ou il rit?

homme   hombre
(hum)
home   ombre
(hum)

white   shite *(hit)*
snake   wake *(ache)*

some   sono   nome *(name)*
noise   meise   soice *(sauce)*

original   rig orinal
     (al   rig!)

juicy
   (you see)

ain't she sweet
    (he's wet)
ain't chees wit
    (he's it)

pigmiss doing a niced hammer shake
in person ate a mid jet named 'clunk
and clank' in a funhouse mirror

pigmiss plain d earlobe calliope, thro
wing it in the blender an elephanb tone,
the tallest mid jet and the shortest jay
ant s hook hands, stin gand tingle
and all t hat

tit o taller thro win turtles at may win doe

I one a hop e bear day
I one a wear a bear is keen
I one a were it
I one address full o fan gels
I ona ass pent my bear day where in it

I one am ache a rah bit this a pear

mother moth
ear the *earth*
th th th th *smooth*
            *smou*th
smooch
th th th

```
e                                    claw

lip            word    tulip      c law

sees       swing   two leaps    sea law

e                                    c low

leap               word's   to leap    c loud

seas                     wing              cloud



I
  am       bla
  amble    bla
  ramble   lack
              bramble     black,
                          the way a woman
                               y a w
                                    o man!
```

unheimliche: an emergency tec
hnique for promoting suffocatio
n by blocking a person's *windpi
pe* by means of a piece of food.

fromage f(rom a)ge

f(eu) (ai)r (eau)o mage

NOTE:

    Say AAAAA... until it turns into an E

    Say EEEEE... until it turns into an I

    Say IIIIIII... until it turns into an O

    Say OOOO... until it turns into an U

    Say "you..." until she turns around

O is the mouth   G is the foot in the mouth

4 is Lemperevr   7 is Le Pendv's nose

(4 + 7 = fourseven = for( )e [11] + venus [17])

down (d = c + l) is shorthand for clown

(therefore, c is a red nose)

NOTE:
Any letter can be expressed as the sum of two other letters in the alphabet
Any trump can be expressed as the sum of two other trumps in the tarot

This is not a preposterous claim, but a claim for preposterity.

fiume (river)
two shapes joined by the finger that traces their contours on the air
(vapore) *fume*

rêves (dreams)

the ability of words to escape our physical and mental control

(reverse) *revés*

NOTE: *if you deliver your answers in the form of riddles you must eat any person who fails to solve them.*

île   Aline

O꜀ᴅ   A line

été   Alain

NOTE: *meaning, Leslie, meaninglessly.*

î   le [île = island]
(d)

vre [(vrai) = true]

oeu

f [(feu) = fire]

NOTE:

oeuf = fueo

fue o

fuego

ego

eg = O

[(fire) = fuego] fue = was/went

go = ir

NOTE TO THE NOTE: once we arrive at an imaginary solution
we ought to find the right imaginary problem for it.

o

ccidental

a

NOTE: Language is a pataphysical web woven by its own exceptions.
when we say "pataphysical" we mean (epi)taphysical, as in the science
that studies the physical properties of epitaphs.

Epitaph = Being turned into letters [(lettre = l'être) after we spill the beans].

Poetry is nothing more than what is embodied in the way P is in B, J is in U,
or V is in X. Who is to say that an E is not an H in profile?

All words are multiversal in that they include/suggest all the other words
that mirror them:

Bee: abeille B an H

Babelle   Bean H

Va belle!   B and H

Babe elle   Band H

Babble   Band age

Babel   Bandage

We write to learn the letters by heart so we can forget what we wrote.

BIT   by   BEET   bye   BEAT:

X and Y   become   Eggs and Whites

NOTE: we are ducks on a pun

we (leave) as if we understand other (peep holes) metaphors,

and in fact we don't
(a nymph act weed on)

all grammars l(e)ake
the letters of a word go e(i)ther way
everybody's tongue sin(g)s

       linguis

            tique

       fantas

cunning linguist

pal(*incestuous*) *mé*(ti)*ssage*

    ho(momo)*phic*

      Momo, king of

           carnival

   cliché

  c(leech)é

  c(leash)é

NOTE:

   Roussel

   Brisset

    - ss

   rouel = roue l = l'roue

   briet = brie t = te brie

(Roussel & Brisset = the whole wheel of cheese)

P.S: to start a fire bend two sticks:

   I I = ( )

and place them between some leaves:

   (feu)illages

Le Son Lenormand

Lenormand *Lesson*
(a game of hope is a game of hoops)

mice + scythe = **myth**

woman + clouds = **woods**

snake + moon = **soon**

garden + moon = **gem**

coffin* + rider = **cider**

garden + sun = **gun**

bear + tree = **tear**

whip + book = **hook**

* this would be the coughing card.

NOTE:

Amateur   Amante   (lover [llover?])

Ama Terre   Amatorio

Am at Air   A mante (mantis/mantia)

WARNING: we don't use cartomancy to write poems but to follow a certain POETIQUETTE.

SORCERY: *S or C, eerie*
(bagatelle = trifle/truffle = Bag Ate Elle [Elle/she ate a bag] = b[agate]lle = bell[e] agate)

SORELLE [S ore(i)lle] = OREILLE = ORILLA
(Soreille = Orilla [ears are sisters] - Oreille = Orilla [ears are shores])

Tal(l)

      Is

           Manic

Trou(t)

        Bad

          (od)Ors

NOTE: Between the tongue and the ear: Larousse/le russe/L.A. ruse/la rose/ arouse UNDER MINING MEANING

sLips:
ecouter est d'écourter l'r
escuchar / *to listen*
       is to cut the air short / es acortar el aire

NOTE: Randomphonic Wordplay Machine

(say it in plains peach)

Word Secrete Secrets

everything but = EVErything/writhing/writing BUTT = Eve writing "butt".

(in a pun two spirits compete for the same body: sound possesses images)

Labile Language, Libel, Labial. Recontre = raconteur = raccoon there!

(l'a-peu-pres)

         Mean
               ing pun
        Smuggl

libro / levres / liebre

Now, okay, everyone say "foule!" (crowd)

No, I mean, everybody say "full!"

Come on, "fool!"

       euphonie = you funny

tw(o) **ins**(ide) [twins   + *iode*]

twins = *miroir* (mirror [me roar]) = *mirar* = to see = *regarder*

      ir ir

                      regar (water up)

                                    = *Soleil*

                    arder (burn up)

NOTE: Logos-n-trick (symboluntary) paraphrenia. Words are:

A means of exchange.

A unit of account.

An instrument of value conservation.

AMUSE YOUR FRIENDS: take the LIP out of OULIPO and go:

Oh! Uh! Oh!

Oh! Oh! Uh!

Uh! Oh! Oh!

(Meth is the future of Myth)

fig. 1:

dAI
rym
AId

fig. 2:

cRO
ssw
ORd

fig. 3:

bIR
TH
RIg
HT

NOTE: When MIRROR becomes the French MIROIR we hear the Spanish MI-RAR (to SEE). In CONTEMPLATION we find a CON, a musing dupe through which we find a TEMPLATe, a pattern that have us focusIng ON the inner sym-metry within a word. Originally a straight line, the word is then turned into a labyrinth in which the eye swerves at the swindle of language turned into its own reflexion.

Auge   (eye)

(belebung)   Auge

NOTE: *just as seeing creates the boom of what is seen, saying something implies taking a chance on what is being said.*

SIDE A:
la bocca della verità

$$mo$$
$$uth$$
$$tr$$

(sempre a schiovere)

SIDE B:
at the end of the ear:

the sound of it all

[rain]

the sound of 'e' tall

[reign]

the sound of feet all   damsel in distress

[wren]

the sound of fetal   dame selling this dress

[wrench]

the sound of Ital(y)

[range]

*D*ice   (to be thrown and used in gambling)

(3ª person singular (él/ella/usted) del verbo decir)   *D*ice

lapel / **no oye** (can't hear/ cant heard?) / lap elle / **noyé** (drowned) / la p(i)el /
neue (new) / l'apelle

NOTE: Parlor Games / Parlare Games
all forms of wordplay can be considered divination as we DIVINE = DIVE INto
a word to be told something by the ripples in it's surface.

ríe
Poétique Curieuse
ri   s

erile
Pu
rsuit

C
unning
P

the daily practice of unexpected happenstances.

A Disposizione

P(rima)

Colazione

(not after Manet)

prosciutto
rosciutto
osciutto   [asciutto = dry]
sciutto
ciutto
iutto   [lutto = mourning]
utto   [tutto = all]
tto
to   [to = take!]
o   (*uovo*)

NOTE: for the anagrammatist, an alphabet is a paupers' boneyard.

spi(RITeS)ong

Défilé = defile

de fille

oblique

lique

lick

t(OUCH)ables

NOTE: SHORTcirCUiT = PrOblEM

phloem

poem

pholems

*(poetic meth
od:
TEXT = SURFACE)*

D(ick)
          iction
Fr(eak)

SIP EAR KIT: all voices will be herded.

```
        S
          ING LE
        J


              CL
        MIRA  E
              G


        C   ZY
          RA
        G   CE


        ea          un
               S

        alt         and


          A   Y
        G WK
          O


          RU
        T   TH
          OO
```

NOTE: "What is writing other than drawing two letters and laughing?"
– Marcel Bénabou

*P*_{our}   (for)

(verser)   *P*_{our}

[the distance between a thing and itself]

verser   for   [flow]
ver   ser   (to see, to be)   f o r   (fire or air)

to tease the heart into beating,
replace the things that were lost
with silence.

pour our p

ver(tir) la mirada

NOTE: *Infinite Intuition + Eternal Perception = gLIMPse*

(some assembly required)

ME*mento***MORY** = hereafter

rafter

tête de mort

Mort

M or T

eM or Tee

Me or Thee

crane

crâne = **skull**   **SKULL** = titanium **WHITE IVORY** black

bird

WH   E

IT

W   HER

eau

cerv

eza

BRAIN = B(e) RAIN

NOTE: a sentence is a distance.

throu ghsh ape

ING
LINGER
  IE

nude
nudo   (knot)
nada   (knothing)   [noticing / not icing / no teasing]

  ING
BE   **INSIDE**
  SIDE

hal fasl eep

MEL   **LY**
    ANCHO
          R

Ban Ana

NOTE:

LIVING THE DREAM   *outwitting females*
in order to provide a better service
I will no longer offer tarot readings
LEAVING THE DREAM   *out wheat, thin females*

```
     M
LE   AT                (tale)
   B    ELEVR          (el verb)
```

```
I        AT   ISE      (étai: [French] on a sailboai, the 'étai' is a line that
                        maintains the mast/le mât forward)
L  MPER   R
```

```
   E      EV           (eve)
```

```
   STOIL               (toils)
LE    LE
   DIAB                (abid: [Arabic] a subordinated, a slave or a servant)
```

```
LA MAIS    DIEV        (mislaid ave)
        ON
   LE M     DE         (led me)
```

```
               L
LA             VNE (navel)
   ROVE DE FORT        (forever dot)
```

NOTE: deaf using the fuzz in defusing (After Jacques Vieville).

BOredOM

NOTE: not all words are available at all times.

ti(**me an**)d (**mean**)ing
ti   d   ing

         eye +
      se **e**ing
       e e
             - y
       e e
             - s ing

            why sing?
            why sign?

            (*Ombre á la Hache = Hombre*)

NOTE:

[an o(pi)nion]:
Spanish vowels often are about two and a half inches bigger than English vowels.

[(a f)act]:

DISCOURSING =
THIS COEUR SING

*tar**occhi***

       occhio

                         *(ocho = **8** = lemnisceight)*

               ojo

                    eye

      trump

            *trompe-l'**oeil***

NOTE: the EYE only exist s in PREsent TENSE.

WARNING: To PIN an OCCHIO is to poke an eye.

```
B EAT
  R   H
EN   ESS
   DL
   I   E
RE   I
   MA N
```

old   ones
Gold and Bones

last as much
as   s uch

Phenomena

Phe n omen a

Fe n omen a

a Fé n omen

a Faith in omen

hi h
g
low

Fascination = 'A' contains 'IF'

NOTE:

linguistick = Ace de Batons

    mi seen scene

outside

        literature

outside

        poetry:

(no insights but in sight)

rejecting
    meaning

    =

rejecting
    value

MONO DE ORGANI

ZAR EL CAOS
SER LE CHAOS

BROYEUR D'ORGANI

     LÈGE
SORTI   JA!
   E

do you do you

     do ʊ do ʊ

                                        [bund(l)es]

doudou?

NOTE: at this point it should be obvious that

'to behave in a cunning manner, so no one will see your brushstroke'
and

   BRU
   SHS. . .
   TROKE

are equivalent operations.

In the beginning, WOrd
pOWer got the
WO
rkfl
OW going.

The sound of a W and an O extended MAN into WOMANand both figured out that there was enough APPLE in hAPPy to make a pie. THE SNAKE was simply another name for THESE NAKED people.

Sun enough, the fLA
gel
LA
tion of the

fLAt
LAnds became a happy song.

NOTE ABOUT CAIN AND ABEL: in CAIN-ABEL we hear CANNIBAL.
Even so (incidentally, EVEN is not "even", but EVE is), we must remember
that to CANE a BELL is to beat a roar.

c   na

ore / oro

sign

ori

nar

c osamenta le

charcuterie:

cha(*)r   *(*i)*

      cut

      (e)erie

NOTE:

alchemy = po(etic hoa)x

to call the soul by another name

hoping that the fools would hear "gold"

NOTE TO THE NOTE:

Zing
      Zing

Bada-Zing

      Boom
Boom:

Man starts with M and woman starts with W.

$M = W$

If one lies on top of the other, you get two diamonds (Try this at home!).

HA HA HA
w   t   s   ppened?

HE   HE
    aven   ll

NOTE:

lumière
        prière de toucher
lui mère
        père rite doucher

                    L   ARGIC
                ETH
                    ER
                                on the edge

                                of the tongue

bewitching
  ew
  we
b   itching
    i ching

                            teased
                              sed = thirst
                                 a thirst for tea

at their best
at hei   st

learnt olive
     learn to live

                i
        in the e ther
                                      l
                              ether
                       n   wor d

               ar   lí
      pe   zi
        ach   tao

NOTE: w(ether) we are talking of planets or words, it all comes down to translation and rotation; where the final frontier can only be boredom.

CAT + WATER = CASTLE
(chat + eau = château)

regno

regnavi   *regnabo*

sum sine regno

regno

ragno

araña

aranya

ra ya

raya

whoever

weaves a line

and understands the difference

between

HERE *and* HERE

UT
    OPIAN
FAL

envidia = **envie** = *envy*

                               ear

       envié = *I sent*   *underw*

                               orld

con

    cunt

coño

    kunst   **BLAS**phemes

                  *ph**ON**emes*

             BLASON

*NOTE: **evil** = **eve ill**.*

<pre>
                        a
                        b
                        o
                        v
                        e
                        s
      similia   similibus
                        o
                        b
                        e
                        l
                        o
                        w
</pre>

s s o a **As so**
e s s i o b i a **I** (will) **be oasis**
v e s s i m o b e l i a **Some**(thing) **is viable**
o v e s s i m i o b e l i l i a **I absolve: I = O simile**
b o v e s s i m i l o b e l o m i l i a **I visible beam, loom soil**
a b o v e s s i m i l i o b e l o w i m i l i a **Blossoms lie: II a womb, I a veil**

NOTE: S BUS = ES BUS = ESBUS = HESHBON = RECKONING

ES

SE   SE

n

SE   CE

bric-

à-brac-

adabrant

NOTE: *n = u*

[elate lit]

1.

Manière de se récréer avec le jeu de cartes nommées tarots

Man

    ière / hiere / wounds

    red / rojo / net

      ser / to be

      écréer / é créer / creer / to believe

        ave / bird

         cle / key

         eje / axis

            de cartes / decartes / Decartes

                art

            nommées tarots / nommé es tar ots

                  no me está roto

           no

           nom / numb

                 star

. 1

Man
wounds net to be (*liebe*
love)

bird key axis

Decartes - art = (deces
decease)

num b is not broken

star

Elate Lit = Etteila = Aliette

thought SUN *said*

refuse t ORO *t*

can one draw a

CIRCLE

CLÉ

from the outside?

v   l
 i   o
  t i
  r

v   3   Al

(bee tree all)

naming a thing makes it subtle

words are a temporary Christ
allization an

IC
on
IC

, clinamatic *le ttriste* song

racole
oracle
aura clé
eau raclé
au ras qu'elle est

breath squeegees gold

*PO*e*T*ry   p*ROSE*

To activate an erotic   gesture a straight line

copulated with a curved line.   In the process of their

lo*BE SO*ng

the alphabet came to be.

[as above so be love]

Appendix

[wanton interlude] a loose chapter on how to use the famous oracle know as "Fortune Cookies"

NOTE: for the oracle to render its full wisdom, at least two or more people should consult it at once. As with the Surrealist's "exquisite corpse", the combined efforts of all the people present will capture the conceptual and immaterial essence of the room.

1) crack the fortune cookie while saying the following prayer:

Chinatown
        pray for us,
Deliver your crispy chicken madness on a Saturday walk
In search for the perfect pork bun, levitating pig heads stare at us with their fried eyes
like little legless ladies we never had the nerve to love and live, captive
in the attic of our remorse.

Chinatown
        pray for us,
Crack the crust of your fried rice uproar on a Saturday walk
Melt your blood into a lead egg roll love, with our kids hoping to kneel down on a golden pancake
worshiping General Tso.

Chinatown
        pray for us,
Sing your monosodium mermaid madness on a Saturday walk
in pagodas crushing coconut buns where we feast our bulletproof bellies on the
wanton quack
hanging upside down.

(Amen)

2) take out the little slip of paper contained inside the cookie (eating the cookie
would be optional).

3) on one side of the slip of paper you will find a message, along with some lot-
tery numbers. Those are a trap for the non-initiate! Ignore them.

4) turn over the slip of paper.

5) on the other side of the slip of paper you will find the inscription LEARN CHI-
NESE accompanied by a word.

    Example:
    hóng luó bo = radish

6) all the seekers must rearrange their slips of paper in such a way that the Chi-
nese words, and their corresponding translations, form a coherent, or semi-co-
herent, whole:

Example 1:
láo jià = excuse me

déng = to wait

zuò ké = be invited

Example 2:
chi = to eat

táo zi = peach

chuí feng = dry hair

Example 3:
tian qì = weather

bíng = disease

ké sóu = to cough

dóu yá = bean sprout

tóu tóng = headache

7) Interpret the message.

WARNING: IT IS EASIER TO VANISH A COIN THAN A THOUGHT.

CPSIA information can be obtained
at www.ICGtesting.com
Printed in the USA
BVHW03s2341080218
507498BV00001B/92/P